Be Thankful for WATER

How Water Sustains our Planet

Harriet Ziefert  Brian Fitzgerald

Red Comet Press • Brooklyn

HARRIET ZIEFERT has written over two hundred books for children. She is also the publisher of Blue Apple Books. She lives and works in the Berkshires, Massachusetts.

BRIAN FITZGERALD is an internationally recognized, award-winning illustrator who lives and works in Ireland.

Library of Congress Control Number: 2022949347
ISBN (HB): 978-1-63655-074-9
ISBN (EBOOK): 978-1-63655-075-6
23 24 25 26 27 TLF 10 9 8 7 6 5 4 3 2 1

First Edition
Printed in China

FSC
www.fsc.org
MIX
Paper from responsible sources
FSC® C104723

RED COMET PRESS   RedCometPress.com

FIRST

Water is home.

Would animals have habitats
without water?

They would not!

Big whales and dolphins,

Sea turtles and sharks,

Octopus, jellyfish,
long eels with sparks.

Shrimp, clams, and oysters,

Fish, seals, and manatee,

Penguins and...

bears live in rivers and seas.

Otters and beavers,

And even some snakes,

Ducks, swans, and hippos
in waterways and lakes.

SECOND

Water is keeping clean.

Could we keep clean
without water?

We could not!

A steamy shower,

A warm, bubbly tub,

A nightly routine—rub-a-dub-dub!

Dishes are sparkling,

Pots looking brand-new,

Clothes, sheets,
and towels
need washing, too!

The car is muddy,
And so is the pet,

Cleaning them means
getting ALL WET!

THIRD

Water is weather.

Would the earth have seasons
without water?

It would not!

A springtime sprinkle,

A summer shower,

A downpour in fall...

with THUNDER power!

Sleet makes streets slushy,

Snow whitens the yard,

Hail bounces around...

ice is slippery hard.

Thick fog is water.

Snowmen—all aglow,

Sun plus water vapor—
a bright rainbow!

Water is recreation.

Would life be fun
without water?

It would not!

Pools for lap swimming,

Ponds for rowboating,

Lazy rivers for paddling and floating.

Canoe in a creek,

Sail on the blue sea,

And on a big lake,
stand on one ski.

Snorkel in the ocean—

What's down
in the deep?

Wave your arms
and take a big leap!

Water is health.

Would our bodies stay healthy
without water?

They would not!

Saliva wets mouths,

Tears moisten our eyes,

Mucus traps germs
of very small size.

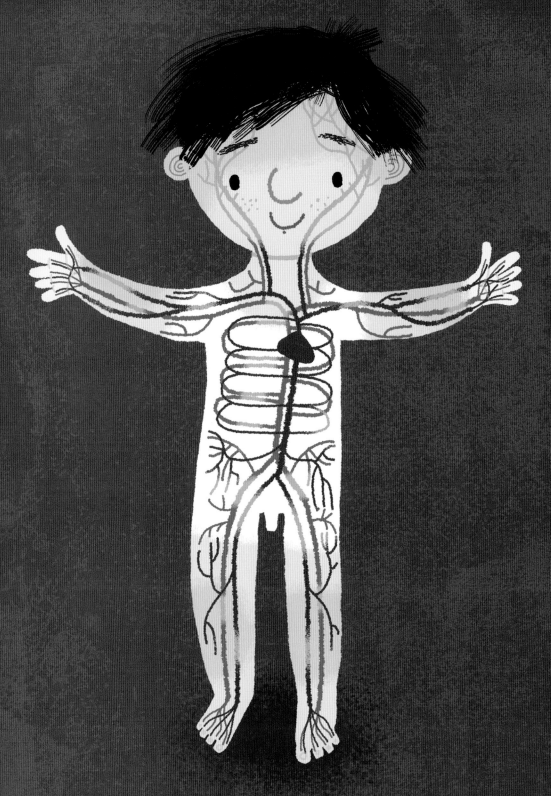

Our bodies' liquids,
Thick ones and thin,

Flush out toxins and
hydrate our skin.

Slurp from a fountain,

Sip from a big cup,

Drinking water helps
to keep your health up!

Water is food.

Would living things be nourished
without water?

They would not!

Grasses for grazers,

Trees for leaf munchers,

Plants for ground snackers,

Bugs for bug munchers.

Seaweed for turtles,
Krill for blue whales,

Algae for crabs and
for little sea snails.

Every size fish
a hungry swimmer,

Everyone likes
a good fish dinner!

Water is life.

Would life be possible
without water?

It would not!

Factory black sludge,
Old plastic galore,

Trash washes up
on the bank and shore.

Trash kills off plants
and sickens the sea,

Let's rid the water of
man-made debris.

Clean oceans and seas,

Pure lakes and rivers,

Healthy living things—
fresh water delivers!

Splash.

Swim.

Surf.

Skate.

Snowboard.

Ski.

Lick a cold ice pop,
Sip some warm tea.

For all of its uses,
Cooled or made hotter,

Always remember,
BE THANKFUL FOR WATER!